filled
WITH
gratitude

My Personal info

- ♥ Name
- ♥ Address
- ♥ Phone
- ♥ Facebook
- ♥ Instagram
- ♥ E-Mail

wake up and be fabulous wake up and be fabulous
Calendar
2021

Su	Mo	Tu	We	Th	Fr	Sa
					1	2
3	4	5	6	7	8	9
10	11	12	13	14	15	16
17	18	19	20	21	22	23
24	25	26	27	28	29	30
31						

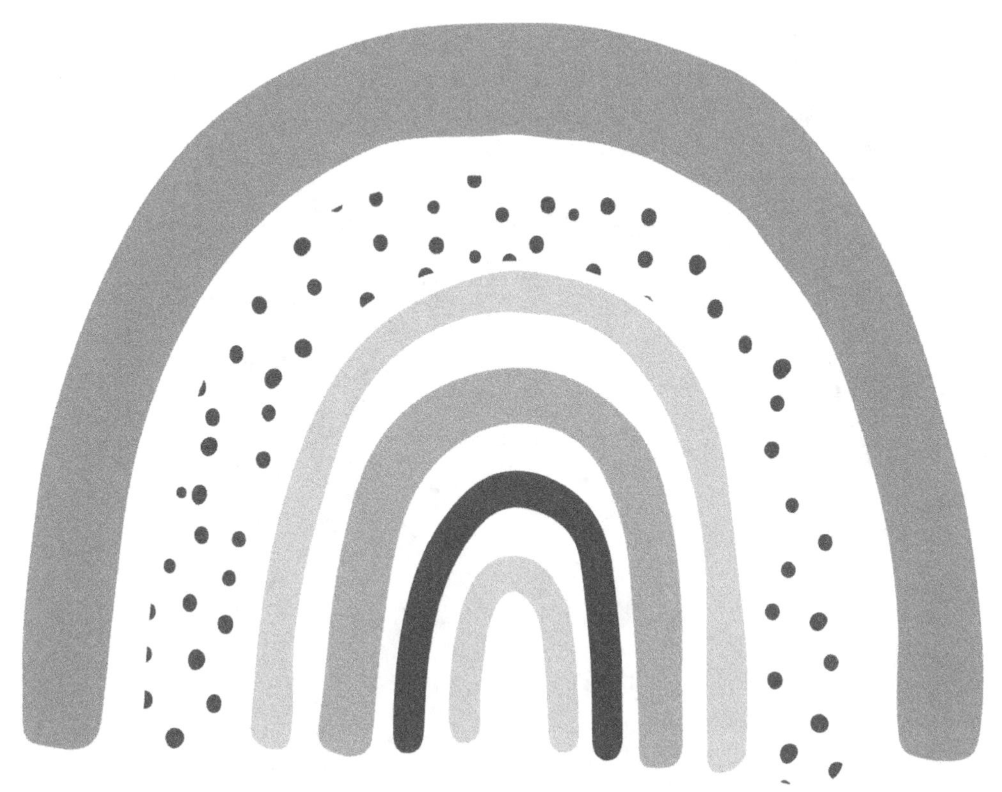

02

FEBRUARY

Su	Mo	Tu	We	Th	Fr	Sa
	1	2	3	4	5	6
7	8	9	10	11	12	13
14	15	16	17	18	19	20
21	22	23	24	25	26	27
28						

03

MARCH

Su	Mo	Tu	We	Th	Fr	Sa
	1	2	3	4	5	6
7	8	9	10	11	12	13
14	15	16	17	18	19	20
21	22	23	24	25	26	27
28	29	30	31			

APRIL

Su	Mo	Tu	We	Th	Fr	Sa
				1	2	3
4	5	6	7	8	9	10
11	12	13	14	15	16	17
18	19	20	21	22	23	24
25	26	27	28	29	30	

05

MAY

Su	Mo	Tu	We	Th	Fr	Sa
						1
2	3	4	5	6	7	8
9	10	11	12	13	14	15
16	17	18	19	20	21	22
23	24	25	26	27	28	29
30	31					

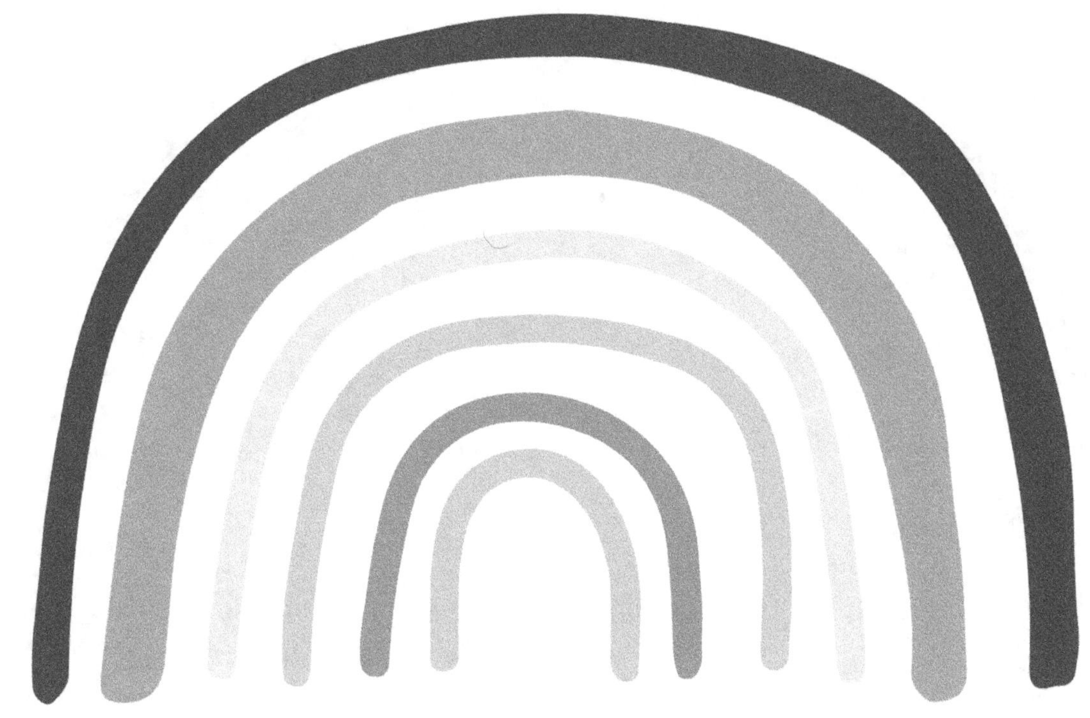

06

JUNE

Su	Mo	Tu	We	Th	Fr	Sa
		1	2	3	4	5
6	7	8	9	10	11	12
13	14	15	16	17	18	19
20	21	22	23	24	25	26
27	28	29	30			

07

JULY

Su	Mo	Tu	We	Th	Fr	Sa
				1	2	3
4	5	6	7	8	9	10
11	12	13	14	15	16	17
18	19	20	21	22	23	24
25	26	27	28	29	30	31

08
AUGUST

Su	Mo	Tu	We	Th	Fr	Sa
1	2	3	4	5	6	7
8	9	10	11	12	13	14
15	16	17	18	19	20	21
22	23	24	25	26	27	28
29	30	31				

09

SEPTEMBER

Su	Mo	Tu	We	Th	Fr	Sa
			1	2	3	4
5	6	7	8	9	10	11
12	13	14	15	16	17	18
19	20	21	22	23	24	25
26	27	28	29	30		

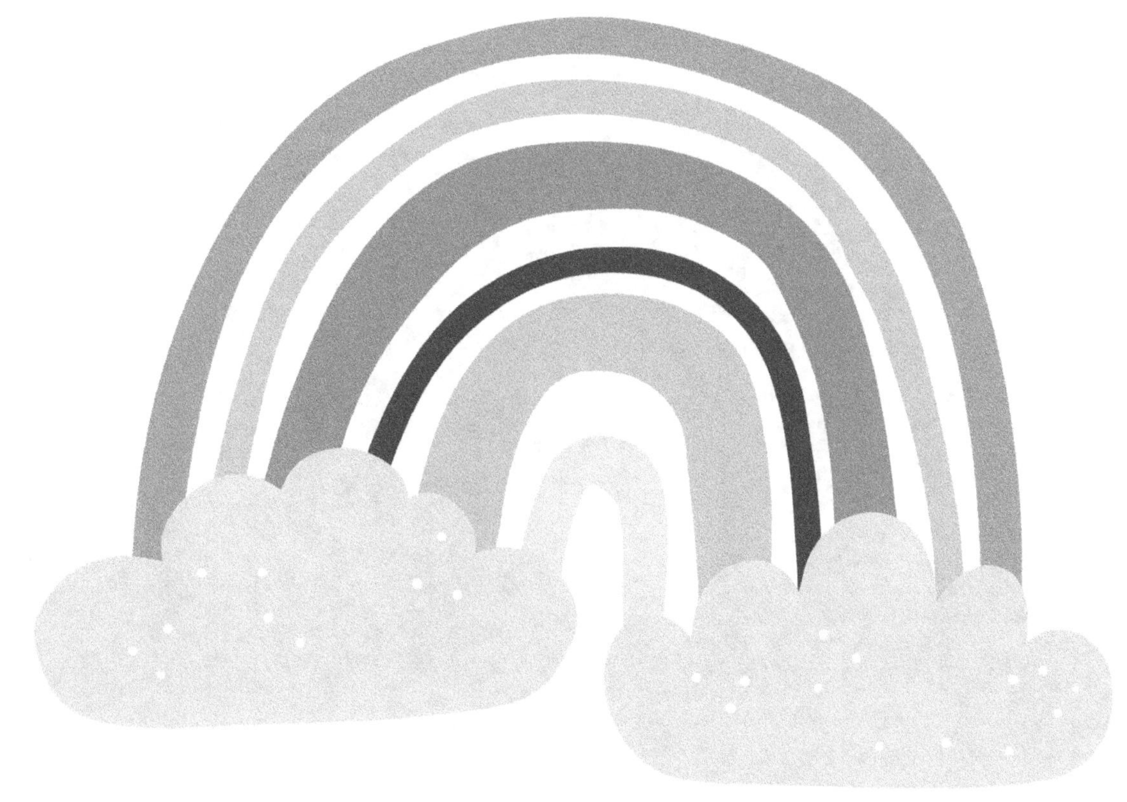

10
OCTOBER

Su	Mo	Tu	We	Th	Fr	Sa
					1	2
3	4	5	6	7	8	9
10	11	12	13	14	15	16
17	18	19	20	21	22	23
24	25	26	27	28	29	30
31						

NOVEMBER

11

Su	Mo	Tu	We	Th	Fr	Sa
	1	2	3	4	5	6
7	8	9	10	11	12	13
14	15	16	17	18	19	20
21	22	23	24	25	26	27
28	29	30				

12

DECEMBER

Su	Mo	Tu	We	Th	Fr	Sa
			1	2	3	4
5	6	7	8	9	10	11
12	13	14	15	16	17	18
19	20	21	22	23	24	25
26	27	28	29	30	31	

MINDFULNESS DAILY JOURNAL

Date: _______/_______/20___

Sun ⬤ | Mon ⬤ | Tue ⬤ | Wed ⬤ | Thu ⬤ | Fri ⬤ | Sat ⬤

IDEAS

MY MOOD TODAY

😊 ☹️ ☹️ 😄 😠

Meditation

How long? _______ / _______

How was it?   Hard ⬤   Easy ⬤

Excercise ⬤   Yoga/Walking/Gym/Other _____________________

Today I Choose to Feel

____
____
____

Today I Will Focus on

____
____
____

Today I feel Inspired By

____
____
____

Good Habits of The Day

____
____
____

To Do List

○ ___________________________
○ ___________________________
○ ___________________________
○ ___________________________
○ ___________________________
○ ___________________________

Today I'm Grateful for

MINDFULNESS DAILY JOURNAL

MY DAY

10 MINUTES TO REFLECT ON YOUR DAY

3 Moments You'd Like To Remember

One Idea of Today That You'd Like To Explore Further

One of The Day's Challenges Big or Small

What I Did Wrong and How To Avoid That

MINDFULNESS DAILY JOURNAL

JOURNAL

goal

MINDFULNESS DAILY JOURNAL

Date: _____ / _____ /20__

Sun Mon Tue Wed Thu Fri Sat

IDEAS

MY MOOD TODAY

Meditation

How long? _____ / _____

How was it?   Hard ◯   Easy ◯

Excercise ◯   Yoga/Walking/Gym/Other ___________________

Today I Choose to Feel

Today I Will Focus on

Today I feel Inspired By

Good Habits of The Day

To Do List

Today I'm Grateful for

MINDFULNESS DAILY JOURNAL

MY DAY

10 MINUTES TO REFLECT ON YOUR DAY

3 Moments You'd Like To Remember

One Idea of Today That You'd Like To Explore Further

One of The Day's Challenges Big or Small

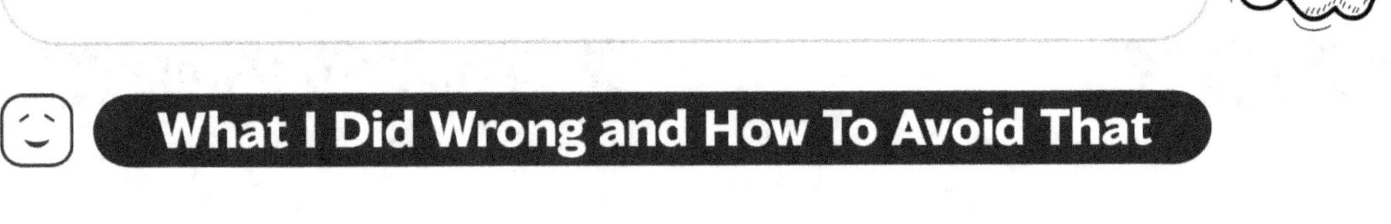

What I Did Wrong and How To Avoid That

MINDFULNESS DAILY JOURNAL

JOURNAL

goal

MINDFULNESS DAILY JOURNAL

Date: _____ / _____ /20__

Sun ◯ Mon ◯ Tue ◯ Wed ◯ Thu ◯ Fri ◯ Sat ◯

IDEAS

MY MOOD TODAY

Today WILL BE A Good Day

Meditation

How long? _____ / _____

How was it? Hard ◯ Easy ◯

Excercise ◯   Yoga/Walking/Gym/Other ________________________

Today I Choose to Feel

Today I Will Focus on

Today I feel Inspired By

Good Habits of The Day

To Do List

Today I'm Grateful for

MINDFULNESS DAILY JOURNAL

MY DAY

10 MINUTES TO REFLECT ON YOUR DAY

3 Moments You'd Like To Remember

One Idea of Today That You'd Like To Explore Further

One of The Day's Challenges Big or Small

What I Did Wrong and How To Avoid That

MINDFULNESS DAILY JOURNAL

JOURNAL

goal

MINDFULNESS DAILY JOURNAL

Date: ______/______/20___

Sun ◯ Mon ◯ Tue ◯ Wed ◯ Thu ◯ Fri ◯ Sat ◯

IDEAS

MY MOOD TODAY

Today WILL BE A Good Day

Meditation

How long? ______ /______

How was it? Hard ◯ Easy ◯

Excercise ◯ Yoga/Walking/Gym/Other ________________

Today I Choose to Feel

Today I Will Focus on

Today I feel Inspired By

Good Habits of The Day

To Do List

Today I'm Grateful for

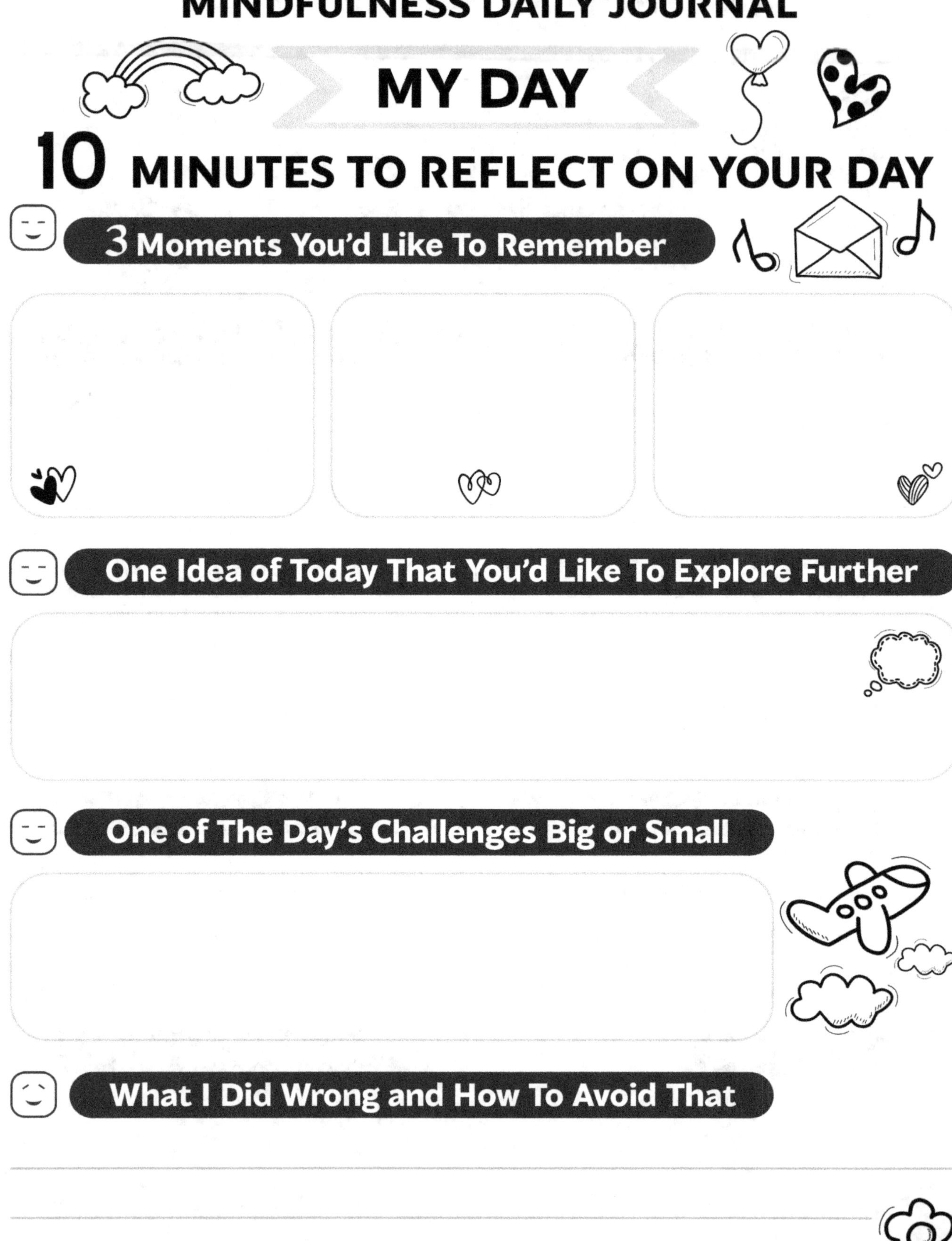

MINDFULNESS DAILY JOURNAL
MY DAY
10 MINUTES TO REFLECT ON YOUR DAY
3 Moments You'd Like To Remember
One Idea of Today That You'd Like To Explore Further
One of The Day's Challenges Big or Small
What I Did Wrong and How To Avoid That

MINDFULNESS DAILY JOURNAL

JOURNAL

goal

MINDFULNESS DAILY JOURNAL

Date: ______/______/20___

Sun ◯ Mon ◯ Tue ◯ Wed ◯ Thu ◯ Fri ◯ Sat ◯

IDEAS

MY MOOD TODAY

Today will be a Good Day

Meditation

How long? ______/______

How was it? Hard ◯ Easy ◯

Excercise ◯ Yoga/Walking/Gym/Other ___________________

Today I Choose to Feel

Today I Will Focus on

Today I feel Inspired By

Good Habits of The Day

To Do List

Today I'm Grateful for

MINDFULNESS DAILY JOURNAL

MY DAY

10 MINUTES TO REFLECT ON YOUR DAY

3 Moments You'd Like To Remember

One Idea of Today That You'd Like To Explore Further

One of The Day's Challenges Big or Small

What I Did Wrong and How To Avoid That

MINDFULNESS DAILY JOURNAL

JOURNAL

goal

MINDFULNESS DAILY JOURNAL

Date: _______/_______/20___

Sun ◯ Mon ◯ Tue ◯ Wed ◯ Thu ◯ Fri ◯ Sat ◯

IDEAS

MY MOOD TODAY

Today WILL BE A Good Day

Meditation

How long? _______ /_______

How was it?   Hard ◯   Easy ◯

Excercise ◯   Yoga/Walking/Gym/Other _______________________

Today I Choose to Feel

____
____
____

Today I Will Focus on

____
____
____

Today I feel Inspired By

____
____
____

Good Habits of The Day

____
____
____

To Do List

◯ _______________________________
◯ _______________________________
◯ _______________________________
◯ _______________________________
◯ _______________________________
◯ _______________________________

Today I'm Grateful for

MINDFULNESS DAILY JOURNAL

MY DAY

10 MINUTES TO REFLECT ON YOUR DAY

3 Moments You'd Like To Remember

One Idea of Today That You'd Like To Explore Further

One of The Day's Challenges Big or Small

What I Did Wrong and How To Avoid That

MINDFULNESS DAILY JOURNAL

JOURNAL

goal

MINDFULNESS DAILY JOURNAL

Date: _______/_______/20___

Sun ◯   Mon ◯   Tue ◯   Wed ◯   Thu ◯   Fri ◯   Sat ◯

IDEAS

MY MOOD TODAY

Today WILL BE A Good Day

Meditation

How long? _______ /_______

How was it?   Hard ◯   Easy ◯

Excercise ◯

Yoga/Walking/Gym/Other _______________________

Today I Choose to Feel

____

____

____

Today I Will Focus on

____

____

____

Today I feel Inspired By

____

____

____

Good Habits of The Day

____

____

____

To Do List

◯ ____________________________________

◯ ____________________________________

◯ ____________________________________

◯ ____________________________________

◯ ____________________________________

◯ ____________________________________

Today I'm Grateful for

MINDFULNESS DAILY JOURNAL

>> MY DAY <<

10 MINUTES TO REFLECT ON YOUR DAY

3 Moments You'd Like To Remember

One Idea of Today That You'd Like To Explore Further

One of The Day's Challenges Big or Small

What I Did Wrong and How To Avoid That

JOURNAL

goal

MINDFULNESS DAILY JOURNAL

Date: _____ / _____ /20___

Sun ◯ Mon ◯ Tue ◯ Wed ◯ Thu ◯ Fri ◯ Sat ◯

IDEAS

MY MOOD TODAY

Meditation

How long? _____ / _____   How was it?   Hard ◯   Easy ◯

Excercise ◯   Yoga/Walking/Gym/Other ___________________

Today I Choose to Feel

Today I Will Focus on

Today I feel Inspired By

Good Habits of The Day

To Do List

Today I'm Grateful for

MINDFULNESS DAILY JOURNAL

MY DAY

10 MINUTES TO REFLECT ON YOUR DAY

3 Moments You'd Like To Remember

One Idea of Today That You'd Like To Explore Further

One of The Day's Challenges Big or Small

What I Did Wrong and How To Avoid That

MINDFULNESS DAILY JOURNAL

JOURNAL

goal

MINDFULNESS DAILY JOURNAL

Date: ______/______/20__

Sun ○   Mon ○   Tue ○   Wed ○   Thu ○   Fri ○   Sat ○

IDEAS

MY MOOD TODAY

☺ ☹ 😐 😄 😠

Today WILL BE A Good Day

Meditation

How long? ______ /______

How was it?   Hard ○   Easy ○

Excercise ○

Yoga/Walking/Gym/Other ____________________

Today I Choose to Feel

____

____

____

Today I Will Focus on

____

____

____

Today I feel Inspired By

____

____

____

Good Habits of The Day

____

____

____

To Do List

○ ______________________________

○ ______________________________

○ ______________________________

○ ______________________________

○ ______________________________

○ ______________________________

Today I'm Grateful for

MINDFULNESS DAILY JOURNAL

MY DAY

10 MINUTES TO REFLECT ON YOUR DAY

3 Moments You'd Like To Remember

One Idea of Today That You'd Like To Explore Further

One of The Day's Challenges Big or Small

What I Did Wrong and How To Avoid That

MINDFULNESS DAILY JOURNAL

JOURNAL

goal

MINDFULNESS DAILY JOURNAL

Date: ______/______/20__

Sun ◯ Mon ◯ Tue ◯ Wed ◯ Thu ◯ Fri ◯ Sat ◯

IDEAS

MY MOOD TODAY

Today WILL BE A Good Day

Meditation

How long? _____ /_____

How was it? Hard ◯ Easy ◯

Excercise ◯   Yoga/Walking/Gym/Other __________________

Today I Choose to Feel

Today I Will Focus on

Today I feel Inspired By

Good Habits of The Day

To Do List

Today I'm Grateful for

MINDFULNESS DAILY JOURNAL

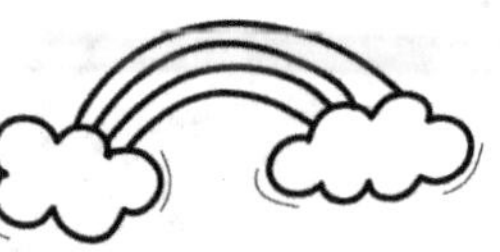

MY DAY

10 MINUTES TO REFLECT ON YOUR DAY

3 Moments You'd Like To Remember

One Idea of Today That You'd Like To Explore Further

One of The Day's Challenges Big or Small

What I Did Wrong and How To Avoid That

MINDFULNESS DAILY JOURNAL

JOURNAL

goal

MINDFULNESS DAILY JOURNAL

Date: _______/_______/20___

Sun ◯ Mon ◯ Tue ◯ Wed ◯ Thu ◯ Fri ◯ Sat ◯

IDEAS

MY MOOD TODAY

Meditation

How long? _______/_______

How was it? Hard ◯ Easy ◯

Excercise ◯   Yoga/Walking/Gym/Other _______________________

Today I Choose to Feel

Today I Will Focus on

Today I feel Inspired By

Good Habits of The Day

To Do List

Today I'm Grateful for

MINDFULNESS DAILY JOURNAL

MY DAY

10 MINUTES TO REFLECT ON YOUR DAY

3 Moments You'd Like To Remember

One Idea of Today That You'd Like To Explore Further

One of The Day's Challenges Big or Small

What I Did Wrong and How To Avoid That

MINDFULNESS DAILY JOURNAL

JOURNAL

goal

MINDFULNESS DAILY JOURNAL

Date: _____/_____/20__

Sun ◯ Mon ◯ Tue ◯ Wed ◯ Thu ◯ Fri ◯ Sat ◯

IDEAS

MY MOOD TODAY

Today WILL BE A Good Day

Meditation

How long? _____/_____

How was it?   Hard ◯   Easy ◯

Excercise ◯   Yoga/Walking/Gym/Other _________________

Today I Choose to Feel

____
____
____

Today I Will Focus on

____
____
____

Today I feel Inspired By

____
____
____

Good Habits of The Day

____
____
____

To Do List

◯ _________________
◯ _________________
◯ _________________
◯ _________________
◯ _________________
◯ _________________

Today I'm Grateful for

MINDFULNESS DAILY JOURNAL

MY DAY

10 MINUTES TO REFLECT ON YOUR DAY

3 Moments You'd Like To Remember

One Idea of Today That You'd Like To Explore Further

One of The Day's Challenges Big or Small

What I Did Wrong and How To Avoid That

MINDFULNESS DAILY JOURNAL

JOURNAL

goal

MINDFULNESS DAILY JOURNAL

Date: _____ / _____ /20__

Sun ◯ Mon ◯ Tue ◯ Wed ◯ Thu ◯ Fri ◯ Sat ◯

IDEAS

MY MOOD TODAY

Today WILL BE A Good Day

Meditation

How long? _____ / _____

How was it? Hard ◯ Easy ◯

Excercise ◯   Yoga/Walking/Gym/Other _________________

Today I Choose to Feel

____
____
____

Today I Will Focus on

____
____
____

Today I feel Inspired By

____
____
____

Good Habits of The Day

____
____
____

To Do List

◯ _______________________
◯ _______________________
◯ _______________________
◯ _______________________
◯ _______________________
◯ _______________________

Today I'm Grateful for

MINDFULNESS DAILY JOURNAL

MY DAY

10 MINUTES TO REFLECT ON YOUR DAY

3 Moments You'd Like To Remember

One Idea of Today That You'd Like To Explore Further

One of The Day's Challenges Big or Small

What I Did Wrong and How To Avoid That

MINDFULNESS DAILY JOURNAL

JOURNAL

goal

MINDFULNESS DAILY JOURNAL

Date: _______/_______/20___

Sun ◯   Mon ◯   Tue ◯   Wed ◯   Thu ◯   Fri ◯   Sat ◯

IDEAS

MY MOOD TODAY

Meditation

How long? _______ /_______

How was it?   Hard ◯   Easy ◯

Excercise ◯   Yoga/Walking/Gym/Other ________________

Today I Choose to Feel

Today I Will Focus on

Today I feel Inspired By

Good Habits of The Day

To Do List

Today I'm Grateful for

MINDFULNESS DAILY JOURNAL

MY DAY

10 MINUTES TO REFLECT ON YOUR DAY

3 Moments You'd Like To Remember

One Idea of Today That You'd Like To Explore Further

One of The Day's Challenges Big or Small

What I Did Wrong and How To Avoid That

MINDFULNESS DAILY JOURNAL

JOURNAL

goal

MINDFULNESS DAILY JOURNAL

Date: _____ / _____ /20__

Sun ◯ Mon ◯ Tue ◯ Wed ◯ Thu ◯ Fri ◯ Sat ◯

IDEAS

MY MOOD TODAY

Meditation

How long? _____ /_____

How was it?   Hard ◯   Easy ◯

Excercise ◯   Yoga/Walking/Gym/Other _________________

Today I Choose to Feel

____
____
____

Today I Will Focus on

____
____
____

Today I feel Inspired By

____
____
____

Good Habits of The Day

____
____
____

To Do List

◯ _______________________
◯ _______________________
◯ _______________________
◯ _______________________
◯ _______________________
◯ _______________________

Today I'm Grateful for

MINDFULNESS DAILY JOURNAL

MY DAY

10 MINUTES TO REFLECT ON YOUR DAY

3 Moments You'd Like To Remember

One Idea of Today That You'd Like To Explore Further

One of The Day's Challenges Big or Small

What I Did Wrong and How To Avoid That

MINDFULNESS DAILY JOURNAL

JOURNAL

MINDFULNESS DAILY JOURNAL

Date: _____/_____/20__

Sun   Mon   Tue   Wed   Thu   Fri   Sat

IDEAS

MY MOOD TODAY

Meditation

How long? _____/_____

How was it?   Hard ◯   Easy ◯

Excercise ◯   Yoga/Walking/Gym/Other _________________

Today I Choose to Feel

Today I Will Focus on

Today I feel Inspired By

Good Habits of The Day

To Do List

Today I'm Grateful for

MINDFULNESS DAILY JOURNAL

MY DAY

10 MINUTES TO REFLECT ON YOUR DAY

3 Moments You'd Like To Remember

One Idea of Today That You'd Like To Explore Further

One of The Day's Challenges Big or Small

What I Did Wrong and How To Avoid That

MINDFULNESS DAILY JOURNAL

JOURNAL

goal

MINDFULNESS DAILY JOURNAL

Date: _____ / _____ /20__

Sun ◯ Mon ◯ Tue ◯ Wed ◯ Thu ◯ Fri ◯ Sat ◯

IDEAS

MY MOOD TODAY

☺ ☹ ☹ 😄 😫

Today WILL BE A Good Day

Meditation

How long? _____ / _____

How was it? Hard ◯ Easy ◯

Excercise ◯   Yoga/Walking/Gym/Other _____________________

Today I Choose to Feel

____
____
____

Today I Will Focus on

____
____
____

Today I feel Inspired By

____
____
____

Good Habits of The Day

____
____
____

To Do List

◯ _______________________
◯ _______________________
◯ _______________________
◯ _______________________
◯ _______________________
◯ _______________________

Today I'm Grateful for

MINDFULNESS DAILY JOURNAL

MY DAY

10 MINUTES TO REFLECT ON YOUR DAY

3 Moments You'd Like To Remember

One Idea of Today That You'd Like To Explore Further

One of The Day's Challenges Big or Small

What I Did Wrong and How To Avoid That

MINDFULNESS DAILY JOURNAL

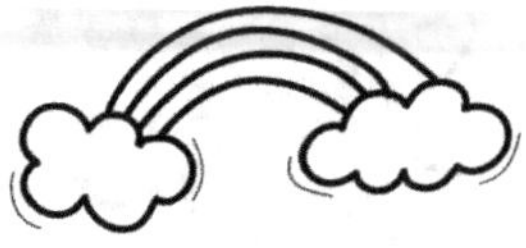  

JOURNAL

goal

MINDFULNESS DAILY JOURNAL

Date: _______/_______/20___

Sun Mon Tue Wed Thu Fri Sat

IDEAS

MY MOOD TODAY

Today WILL BE A Good Day

Meditation

How long? _______ /_______

How was it?   Hard ◯   Easy ◯

Excercise ◯   Yoga/Walking/Gym/Other ____________________

Today I Choose to Feel

Today I Will Focus on

Today I feel Inspired By

Good Habits of The Day

To Do List

Today I'm Grateful for

MINDFULNESS DAILY JOURNAL

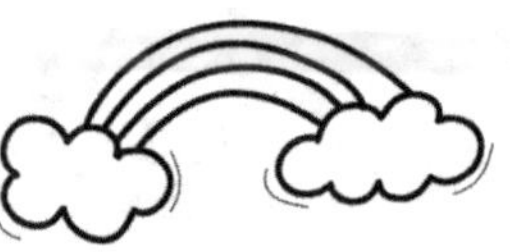

MY DAY

10 MINUTES TO REFLECT ON YOUR DAY

3 Moments You'd Like To Remember

One Idea of Today That You'd Like To Explore Further

One of The Day's Challenges Big or Small

What I Did Wrong and How To Avoid That

MINDFULNESS DAILY JOURNAL

JOURNAL

goal

MINDFULNESS DAILY JOURNAL

Date: _____/_____/20__

Sun ○   Mon ○   Tue ○   Wed ○   Thu ○   Fri ○   Sat ○

IDEAS

MY MOOD TODAY

Today WILL BE A Good Day

Meditation

How long? _____ /_____   How was it?   Hard ○   Easy ○

Excercise ○   Yoga/Walking/Gym/Other ___________________

Today I Choose to Feel

____
____
____

Today I Will Focus on

____
____
____

Today I feel Inspired By

____
____
____

Good Habits of The Day

____
____
____

To Do List

○ ___________________
○ ___________________
○ ___________________
○ ___________________
○ ___________________
○ ___________________

Today I'm Grateful for

MINDFULNESS DAILY JOURNAL

MY DAY

10 MINUTES TO REFLECT ON YOUR DAY

3 Moments You'd Like To Remember

One Idea of Today That You'd Like To Explore Further

One of The Day's Challenges Big or Small

What I Did Wrong and How To Avoid That

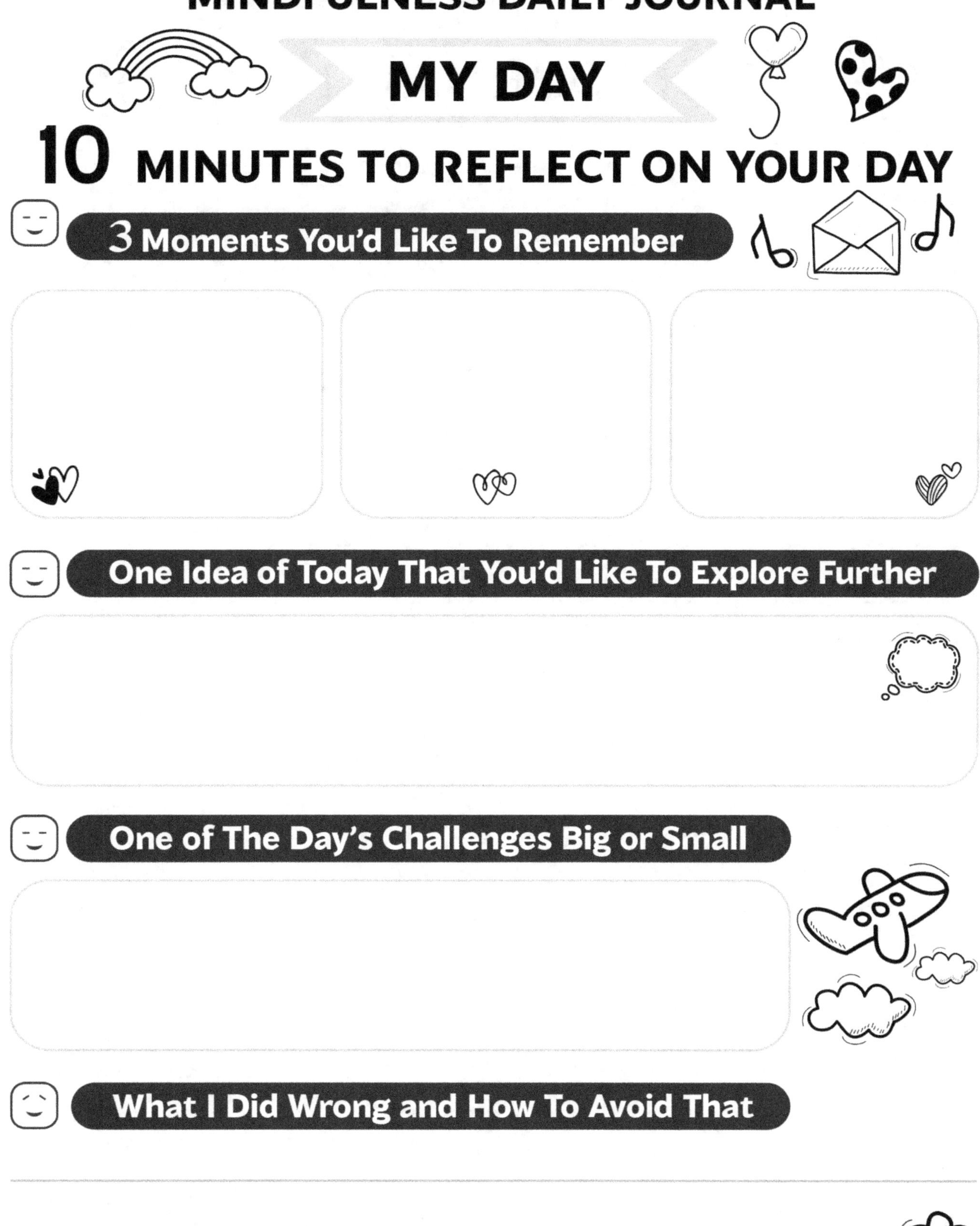

MINDFULNESS DAILY JOURNAL

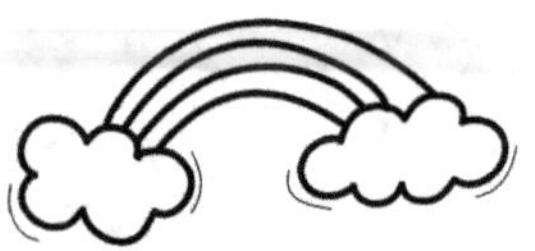

JOURNAL

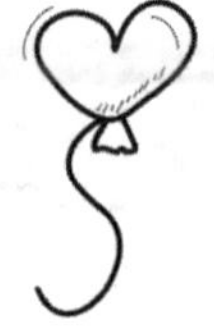

goal

MINDFULNESS DAILY JOURNAL

Date: _____ / _____ /20__

Sun ◯ Mon ◯ Tue ◯ Wed ◯ Thu ◯ Fri ◯ Sat ◯

IDEAS

MY MOOD TODAY

😊 ☹️ 😐 😄 😠

Today WILL BE A Good Day

Meditation

How long? _____ / _____

How was it? Hard ◯ Easy ◯

Excercise ◯   Yoga/Walking/Gym/Other _____________________

Today I Choose to Feel

____
____
____

Today I Will Focus on

____
____
____

Today I feel Inspired By

____
____
____

Good Habits of The Day

____
____
____

To Do List

◯ _______________________
◯ _______________________
◯ _______________________
◯ _______________________
◯ _______________________
◯ _______________________

Today I'm Grateful for

MINDFULNESS DAILY JOURNAL

MY DAY

10 MINUTES TO REFLECT ON YOUR DAY

3 Moments You'd Like To Remember

One Idea of Today That You'd Like To Explore Further

One of The Day's Challenges Big or Small

What I Did Wrong and How To Avoid That

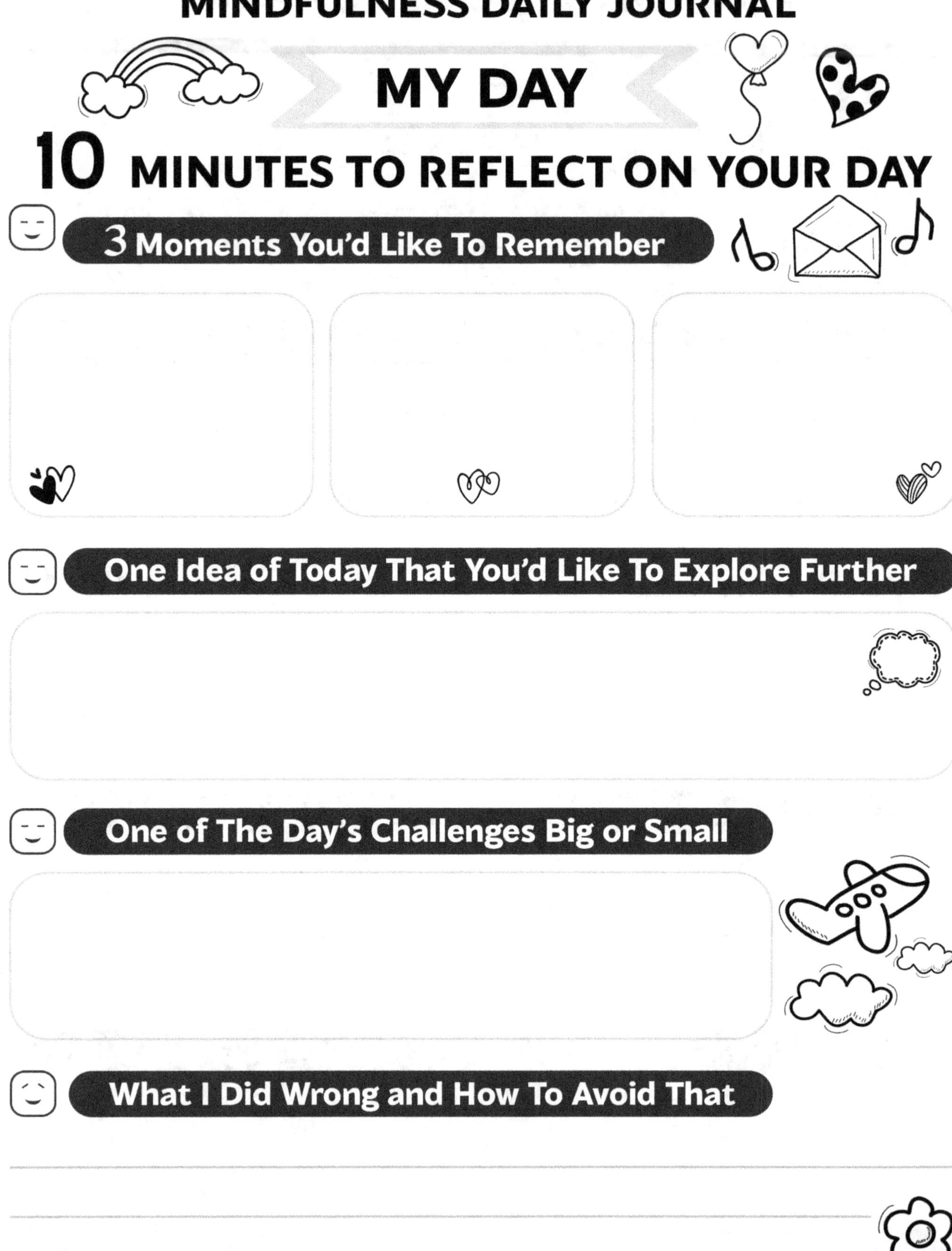

MINDFULNESS DAILY JOURNAL

JOURNAL

goal

MINDFULNESS DAILY JOURNAL

Date: _____/_____/20__

Sun ◯ Mon ◯ Tue ◯ Wed ◯ Thu ◯ Fri ◯ Sat ◯

IDEAS

MY MOOD TODAY

Today WILL BE A Good Day

Meditation

How long? _____/_____

How was it?   Hard ◯   Easy ◯

Excercise ◯   Yoga/Walking/Gym/Other _________________

Today I Choose to Feel

____

____

____

Today I Will Focus on

____

____

____

Today I feel Inspired By

____

____

____

Good Habits of The Day

____

____

____

To Do List

◯ _______________________

◯ _______________________

◯ _______________________

◯ _______________________

◯ _______________________

◯ _______________________

Today I'm Grateful for

MINDFULNESS DAILY JOURNAL

MY DAY

10 MINUTES TO REFLECT ON YOUR DAY

3 Moments You'd Like To Remember

One Idea of Today That You'd Like To Explore Further

One of The Day's Challenges Big or Small

What I Did Wrong and How To Avoid That

MINDFULNESS DAILY JOURNAL

JOURNAL

goal

MINDFULNESS DAILY JOURNAL

Date: _____ / _____ /20___

Sun ◯ Mon ◯ Tue ◯ Wed ◯ Thu ◯ Fri ◯ Sat ◯

IDEAS

MY MOOD TODAY

Meditation

How long? _____ / _____

How was it? Hard ◯ Easy ◯

Excercise ◯   Yoga/Walking/Gym/Other _______________

Today I Choose to Feel

Today I Will Focus on

Today I feel Inspired By

Good Habits of The Day

To Do List

Today I'm Grateful for

MINDFULNESS DAILY JOURNAL

MY DAY

10 MINUTES TO REFLECT ON YOUR DAY

3 Moments You'd Like To Remember

One Idea of Today That You'd Like To Explore Further

One of The Day's Challenges Big or Small

What I Did Wrong and How To Avoid That

MINDFULNESS DAILY JOURNAL

 ## JOURNAL  

goal

MINDFULNESS DAILY JOURNAL

Date: _____/_____/20__

Sun Mon Tue Wed Thu Fri Sat

IDEAS

MY MOOD TODAY

Today WILL BE A Good Day

Meditation

How long? _____ /_____   How was it?   Hard ◯   Easy ◯

Excercise ◯   Yoga/Walking/Gym/Other ________________

Today I Choose to Feel

Today I Will Focus on

Today I feel Inspired By

Good Habits of The Day

To Do List

Today I'm Grateful for

MINDFULNESS DAILY JOURNAL

MY DAY

10 MINUTES TO REFLECT ON YOUR DAY

3 Moments You'd Like To Remember

One Idea of Today That You'd Like To Explore Further

One of The Day's Challenges Big or Small

What I Did Wrong and How To Avoid That

MINDFULNESS DAILY JOURNAL

 ## JOURNAL 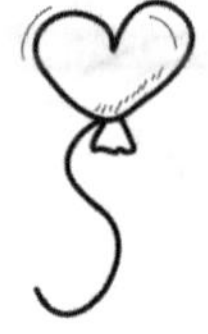 

goal

MINDFULNESS DAILY JOURNAL

Date: _____ / _____ /20__

Sun ○ Mon ○ Tue ○ Wed ○ Thu ○ Fri ○ Sat ○

IDEAS

MY MOOD TODAY

☺ ☹ ☹ 😄 😠

Today WILL BE A Good Day

Meditation

How long? _____ / _____

How was it?   Hard ○   Easy ○

Excercise ○   Yoga/Walking/Gym/Other ___________________

Today I Choose to Feel

____

____

____

Today I Will Focus on

____

____

____

Today I feel Inspired By

____

____

____

Good Habits of The Day

____

____

____

To Do List

○ _______________________
○ _______________________
○ _______________________
○ _______________________
○ _______________________
○ _______________________

Today I'm Grateful for

GRATITUDE

MINDFULNESS DAILY JOURNAL

MY DAY

10 MINUTES TO REFLECT ON YOUR DAY

3 Moments You'd Like To Remember

One Idea of Today That You'd Like To Explore Further

One of The Day's Challenges Big or Small

What I Did Wrong and How To Avoid That

MINDFULNESS DAILY JOURNAL

 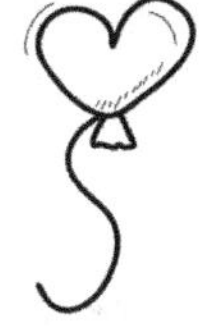 

JOURNAL

goal

MINDFULNESS DAILY JOURNAL

Date: _______/_______/20___

Sun ◯ Mon ◯ Tue ◯ Wed ◯ Thu ◯ Fri ◯ Sat ◯

MY MOOD TODAY

IDEAS

☺ ☹ ☹ 😄 😠

Today WILL BE A Good Day

Meditation

How long? _______/_______

How was it? Hard ◯ Easy ◯

Excercise ◯

Yoga/Walking/Gym/Other _______________________

Today I Choose to Feel

____

____

Today I Will Focus on

____

____

Today I feel Inspired By

____

____

Good Habits of The Day

____

____

To Do List

◯ _______________________________

◯ _______________________________

◯ _______________________________

◯ _______________________________

◯ _______________________________

◯ _______________________________

Today I'm Grateful for

MINDFULNESS DAILY JOURNAL

MY DAY

10 MINUTES TO REFLECT ON YOUR DAY

3 Moments You'd Like To Remember

One Idea of Today That You'd Like To Explore Further

One of The Day's Challenges Big or Small

What I Did Wrong and How To Avoid That

MINDFULNESS DAILY JOURNAL

JOURNAL

goal

MINDFULNESS DAILY JOURNAL

Date: _____ / _____ /20__

Sun ◯ Mon ◯ Tue ◯ Wed ◯ Thu ◯ Fri ◯ Sat ◯

IDEAS

MY MOOD TODAY

☺ ☹ ☹ 😄 😠

Today WILL BE A Good Day

Meditation

How long? _____ / _____

How was it? Hard ◯ Easy ◯

Excercise ◯ Yoga/Walking/Gym/Other ___________________

Today I Choose to Feel

____
____
____

Today I Will Focus on

____
____
____

Today I feel Inspired By

____
____
____

Good Habits of The Day

____
____
____

To Do List

◯ _______________________
◯ _______________________
◯ _______________________
◯ _______________________
◯ _______________________
◯ _______________________

Today I'm Grateful for

MINDFULNESS DAILY JOURNAL

MY DAY

10 MINUTES TO REFLECT ON YOUR DAY

3 Moments You'd Like To Remember

One Idea of Today That You'd Like To Explore Further

One of The Day's Challenges Big or Small

What I Did Wrong and How To Avoid That

MINDFULNESS DAILY JOURNAL

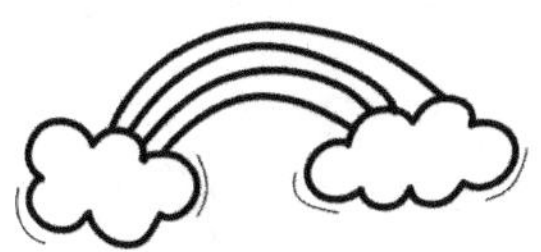

JOURNAL

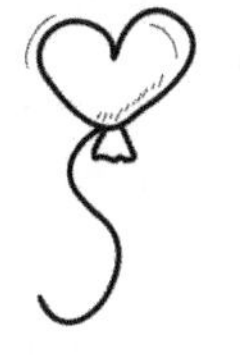

goal

MINDFULNESS DAILY JOURNAL

Date: _____ / _____ /20___

Sun ◯ Mon ◯ Tue ◯ Wed ◯ Thu ◯ Fri ◯ Sat ◯

IDEAS

MY MOOD TODAY

Today WILL BE A Good Day

Meditation

How long? _____ / _____

How was it? Hard ◯ Easy ◯

Excercise ◯

Yoga/Walking/Gym/Other _________________

Today I Choose to Feel

____
____
____

Today I Will Focus on

____
____
____

Today I feel Inspired By

____
____
____

Good Habits of The Day

____
____
____

To Do List

◯ _______________________
◯ _______________________
◯ _______________________
◯ _______________________
◯ _______________________
◯ _______________________

Today I'm Grateful for

MINDFULNESS DAILY JOURNAL

MY DAY

10 MINUTES TO REFLECT ON YOUR DAY

3 Moments You'd Like To Remember

One Idea of Today That You'd Like To Explore Further

One of The Day's Challenges Big or Small

What I Did Wrong and How To Avoid That

MINDFULNESS DAILY JOURNAL

JOURNAL

goal

MINDFULNESS DAILY JOURNAL

Date: _____ / _____ /20__

Sun Mon Tue Wed Thu Fri Sat

IDEAS

MY MOOD TODAY

Today WILL BE A Good Day

Meditation

How long? _____ / _____

How was it? Hard ◯ Easy ◯

Excercise ◯ Yoga/Walking/Gym/Other _________________

Today I Choose to Feel

____

____

____

Today I Will Focus on

____

____

____

Today I feel Inspired By

____

____

____

Good Habits of The Day

____

____

____

To Do List

◯ ________________________

◯ ________________________

◯ ________________________

◯ ________________________

◯ ________________________

◯ ________________________

Today I'm Grateful for

GRATITUDE

MINDFULNESS DAILY JOURNAL

MY DAY

10 MINUTES TO REFLECT ON YOUR DAY

3 Moments You'd Like To Remember

One Idea of Today That You'd Like To Explore Further

One of The Day's Challenges Big or Small

What I Did Wrong and How To Avoid That

MINDFULNESS DAILY JOURNAL

JOURNAL

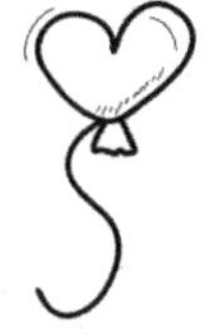

goal

MINDFULNESS DAILY JOURNAL

Date: _____/_____/20__

Sun◯ Mon◯ Tue◯ Wed◯ Thu◯ Fri◯ Sat◯

IDEAS

MY MOOD TODAY

Meditation

How long? _____ /_____

How was it? Hard ◯ Easy ◯

Excercise ◯ Yoga/Walking/Gym/Other __________________

Today I Choose to Feel

Today I Will Focus on

Today I feel Inspired By

Good Habits of The Day

To Do List

Today I'm Grateful for

MINDFULNESS DAILY JOURNAL

MY DAY

10 MINUTES TO REFLECT ON YOUR DAY

3 Moments You'd Like To Remember

One Idea of Today That You'd Like To Explore Further

One of The Day's Challenges Big or Small

What I Did Wrong and How To Avoid That

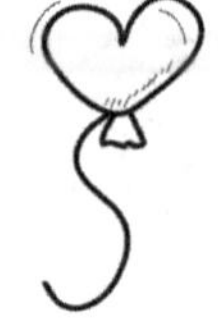

JOURNAL

goal

MINDFULNESS DAILY JOURNAL

Date: _______/_______/20___

Sun ◯ Mon ◯ Tue ◯ Wed ◯ Thu ◯ Fri ◯ Sat ◯

IDEAS

MY MOOD TODAY

😊 ☹️ 😠 😄 😡

Today WILL BE A Good Day

Meditation

How long? _______/_______

How was it? Hard ◯ Easy ◯

Excercise ◯

Yoga/Walking/Gym/Other ___________________

Today I Choose to Feel

____
____
____

Today I Will Focus on

____
____
____

Today I feel Inspired By

____
____
____

Good Habits of The Day

____
____
____

To Do List

◯ _______________________
◯ _______________________
◯ _______________________
◯ _______________________
◯ _______________________
◯ _______________________

Today I'm Grateful for

MINDFULNESS DAILY JOURNAL

MY DAY

10 MINUTES TO REFLECT ON YOUR DAY

3 Moments You'd Like To Remember

One Idea of Today That You'd Like To Explore Further

One of The Day's Challenges Big or Small

What I Did Wrong and How To Avoid That

JOURNAL

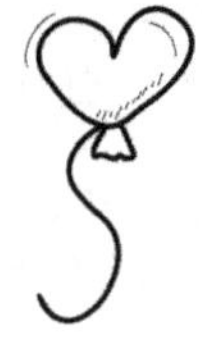

goal

MINDFULNESS DAILY JOURNAL

Date: _____ / _____ /20___

Sun ◯ Mon ◯ Tue ◯ Wed ◯ Thu ◯ Fri ◯ Sat ◯

IDEAS

MY MOOD TODAY

Today WILL BE A Good Day

Meditation

How long? _____ /_____

How was it? Hard ◯ Easy ◯

Excercise ◯

Yoga/Walking/Gym/Other ___________________

Today I Choose to Feel

____
____
____

Today I Will Focus on

____
____
____

Today I feel Inspired By

____
____
____

Good Habits of The Day

____
____
____

To Do List

- ◯ ______________________________
- ◯ ______________________________
- ◯ ______________________________
- ◯ ______________________________
- ◯ ______________________________
- ◯ ______________________________

Today I'm Grateful for

MINDFULNESS DAILY JOURNAL

MY DAY

10 MINUTES TO REFLECT ON YOUR DAY

3 Moments You'd Like To Remember

One Idea of Today That You'd Like To Explore Further

One of The Day's Challenges Big or Small

What I Did Wrong and How To Avoid That

MINDFULNESS DAILY JOURNAL

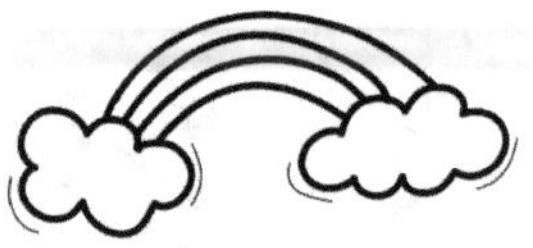

JOURNAL

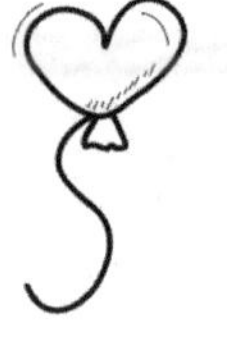 

goal

MINDFULNESS DAILY JOURNAL

Date: _____ / _____ /20__

Sun Mon Tue Wed Thu Fri Sat

IDEAS

MY MOOD TODAY

Meditation

How long? _____ / _____

How was it?   Hard ◯   Easy ◯

Excercise ◯   Yoga/Walking/Gym/Other _________________

Today I Choose to Feel

Today I Will Focus on

Today I feel Inspired By

Good Habits of The Day

To Do List

Today I'm Grateful for

MINDFULNESS DAILY JOURNAL

MY DAY

10 MINUTES TO REFLECT ON YOUR DAY

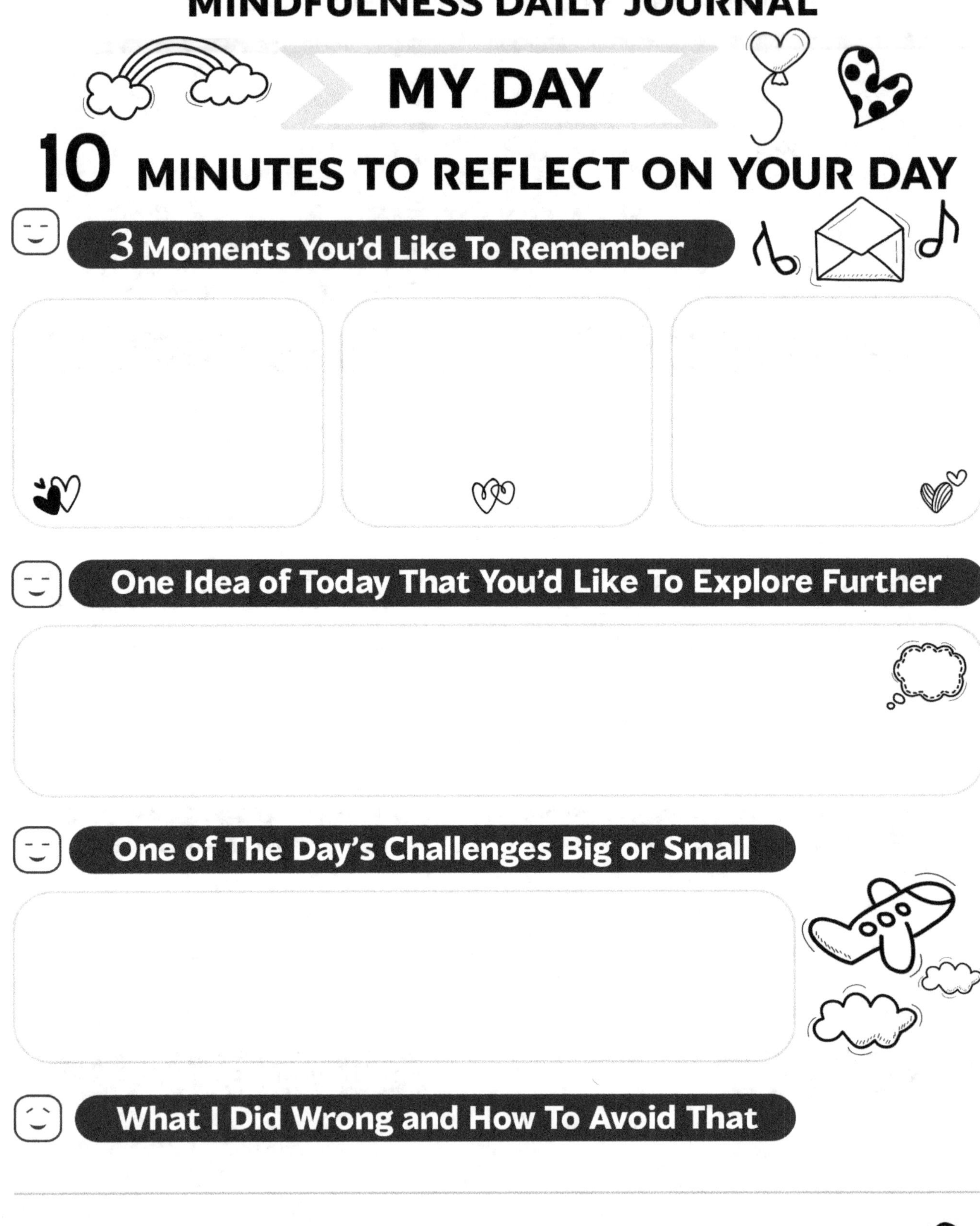

3 Moments You'd Like To Remember

One Idea of Today That You'd Like To Explore Further

One of The Day's Challenges Big or Small

What I Did Wrong and How To Avoid That

MINDFULNESS DAILY JOURNAL

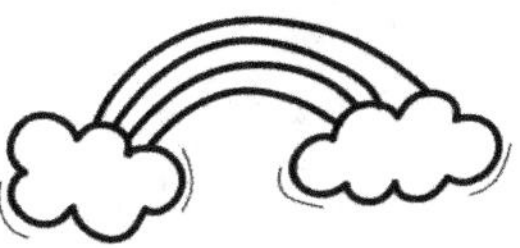 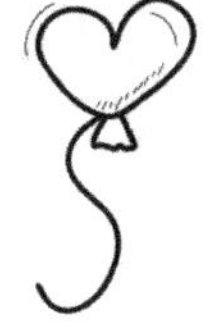 

JOURNAL

goal

Journal

MINDFULNESS DAILY JOURNAL

JOURNAL

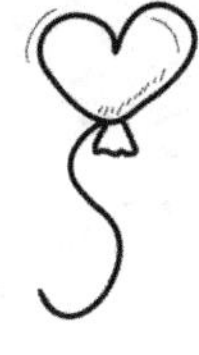

goal

MINDFULNESS DAILY JOURNAL

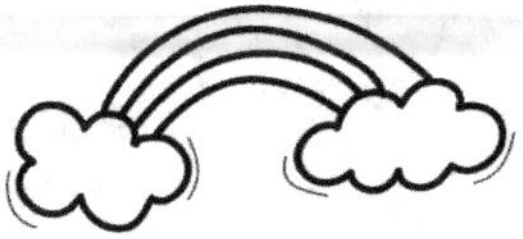 ## JOURNAL  

goal

MINDFULNESS DAILY JOURNAL

JOURNAL

goal

# MINDFULNESS DAILY JOURNAL

JOURNAL

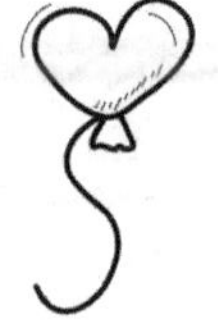

goal

MINDFULNESS DAILY JOURNAL

JOURNAL

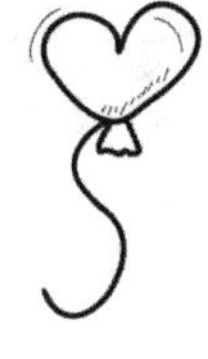

goal

MINDFULNESS DAILY JOURNAL

JOURNAL

MINDFULNESS DAILY JOURNAL

JOURNAL

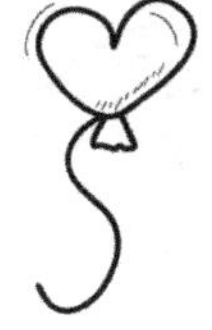

goal

MINDFULNESS DAILY JOURNAL

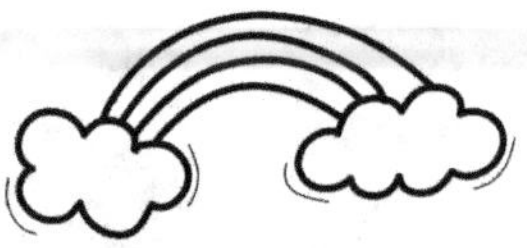 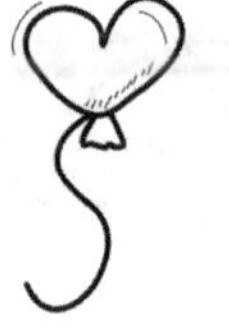 

JOURNAL

goal

MINDFULNESS DAILY JOURNAL

 ## JOURNAL  

goal

MINDFULNESS DAILY JOURNAL

 **JOURNAL**  

goal

MINDFULNESS DAILY JOURNAL

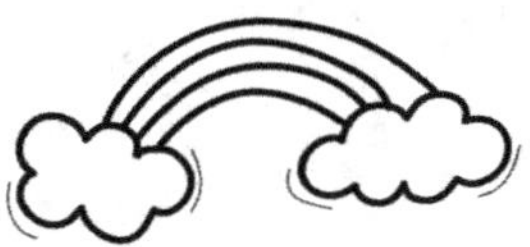

JOURNAL

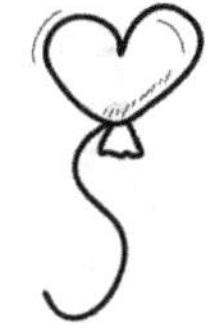

goal

MINDFULNESS DAILY JOURNAL

JOURNAL

goal

MINDFULNESS DAILY JOURNAL

JOURNAL

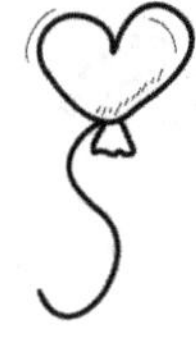

goal

MINDFULNESS DAILY JOURNAL

JOURNAL

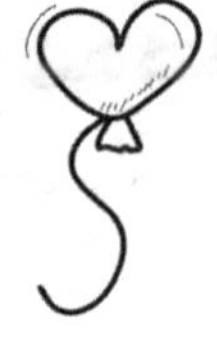

goal

MINDFULNESS DAILY JOURNAL

JOURNAL

goal

MINDFULNESS DAILY JOURNAL

JOURNAL

goal

MINDFULNESS DAILY JOURNAL

JOURNAL

goal

MINDFULNESS DAILY JOURNAL

JOURNAL

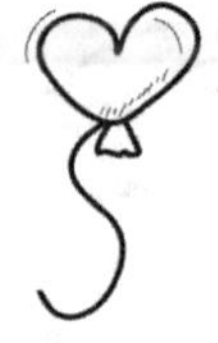

goal

MINDFULNESS DAILY JOURNAL

JOURNAL

goal

MINDFULNESS DAILY JOURNAL

JOURNAL

goal

MINDFULNESS DAILY JOURNAL

JOURNAL

goal

MINDFULNESS DAILY JOURNAL

JOURNAL

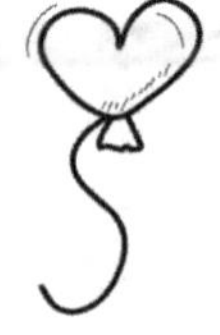

goal

MINDFULNESS DAILY JOURNAL

JOURNAL

goal

JOURNAL

goal

MINDFULNESS DAILY JOURNAL

JOURNAL

goal

MINDFULNESS DAILY JOURNAL

JOURNAL

goal

MINDFULNESS DAILY JOURNAL

JOURNAL

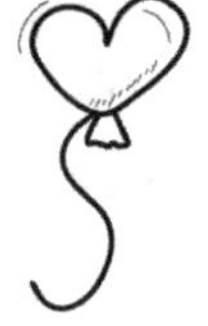

goal

MINDFULNESS DAILY JOURNAL

JOURNAL

goal